An Improved Sabre Exercise

A Historical Military Article Containing Instructions in Fencing for Mounted and Dismounted Service

By

H R Hershberger

British Library Cataloguing-in-Publication Data
A catalogue record for this book is available from
the British Library

AN

IMPROVED SABRE EXERCISE.

CONTAINING

INSTRUCTIONS IN FENCING

FOR

MOUNTED AND DISMOUNTED SERVICE.

RULES FOR THE SABRE EXERCISE IN THE SADDLE.

Section I.—*Cuts.*

THERE are only seven ways of directing the edge of the sabre.

The action of the wrist and shoulder alone should direct the blade; but the elbow may sometimes be a little bent (with safety) to give more force to the cut, thrust, or parry, particularly when acting against INFANTRY.

Of the seven cuts, four are made diagonally, two horizontally, and one perpendicularly.

The cuts *three* and *four* should not be made in *mounted service*, except with the greatest caution; for, as in making those cuts, the body is somewhat unavoidably exposed, your adversary (if well acquainted with the science) will ever be ready to take advantage of such exposure: he will cause *openings* to induce an attack at those *points*, as a cut at the sword arm or bridle arm can be made with the greatest security, and, if well directed, with most fatal effect; and it at once decides the issue of the contest.

The edge of the sabre should lead in whatever direction the cut is intended.

Every cut should be made with the sabre drawn toward you about an inch, lest it should not prove a *cut*.

It should be remembered that every cut made, exposes more or less of the body, and you should always be ready to guard the part exposed.

To enable you to understand the direction of the blade in the cuts, you should have a board about two feet square, and lines marked upon it, thus:

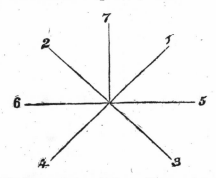

At the different points of these lines, place the figures as above represented.

Each cut is to commence at its respective figure and terminate at the centre, where the lines cross one another.

From the want of habit in the exercise of the wrist in the common occupations of life, the use of the sabre will, at first, be found extremely tiresome; and hence the closest perseverance will be necessary to attain perfection in the first lessons, which are *merely* for the purpose of acquiring suppleness in the wrist and shoulder, and to bring those muscles of the arm into action which give the weaker man (if a swordsman) a decided advantage over the stronger, if unaccustomed to the use of the weapon.

Section II.—*Guards.*

There should be but *three* guards used, either in mounted or dismounted service; and those guards, with very little variation, will receive *all cuts* that can be made.

The *first guard* is nearly horizontal, the arm extended and hand higher than the head—the edge of the sabre up and a little inclined to the front—the point to the left front and about six higher than the hilt. This guard can be made at any point from the left rear to the rear, and will protect against cut *seven*.

As an unerring rule, keep the sword hand directed toward your antagonist's left ear (*eying* him under the sabre) lest he takes advantage of your sword arm.

The *second guard* is a hanging guard to the left side of the body, hand higher than the head, edge to the left, point of the sabre a little out to the left front, and the arm at the full extent.

In the hanging guards, you are able to protect yourself and horse by varying them quicker than your adversary can possibly give the cuts. As the formation of these *guards* is very simple and effective, they can be made with more safety, more ease, and quicker than the guards of any other broad-sword system.

The *third guard* is also a hanging guard, formed by extending the arm to the right front, hand higher than the head, edge out, and sabre nearly vertical. This *guard*, when correctly made, will, with but little variation, protect against cuts *two, four*, and *six ;* and if extended to the right rear, will save yourself and horse from any of the above named *cuts*.

All guards should be made at the full extent of the arm.

If the guards are made close to the body, they are liable to become *broken*, and you may still receive the cut; but the further the guards are extended, the further the antagonist is kept off.

In the hanging guards—numbers *two* and *three*—the point of the sabre is sometimes thrown out or in, according as the cuts are made.

In forming the *second* and *third* guards, it matters not what your position may be in the saddle, they can be named at whatever point they are made. For instance: if you extend the arm to the front, it is called the front hanging guard; if to the right front, the right front hanging guard, and so on, until the guard is formed entirely around you; and it can be made at any point from the left rear to the rear, raising the point of the sabre over the horse's neck.

It is to be supposed that, in *single* combat, swordsmen will meet sword arm to sword arm; they will then be on equal footing as regards position.

It seldom happens (unless through exceedingly bad

horsemanship) that a person is ever attacked *singly* at his " weak quarter," *i. e.*, his left rear. He will have sufficient time to turn his horse " about" and receive his antagonist ; but, if outnumbered in pursuit, he should draw pistol and fire at his pursuer, under his bridle arm, to the left rear, before he gets within reach with his sabre. After firing, he should immediately gather his sabre, and, if possible, turn to the " right-about."

If your adversary passes you, which he would not do if a swordsman, pursue and attack him at the same point, *i. e.*, the left rear.

The attack should not be made on the left side, except against *Infantry ;* for your opponent has the advantage of nearly the breadth of your chest, and quite so, if to the left rear.

Section III.—*Points.*

There should be but two points used.

The *first point* is made by drawing back the sabre so that the back of the hand will be about two inches from the right cheek, the hilt firmly grasped, edge up, and point toward your antagonist.

The *second point* is used in pursuit, and made at the left rear or " weak quarter;" it is formed by drawing back the hand on the right hip, basket or guard covering the back of the hand, edge up, and point as high as the shoulder.

The greatest caution must be observed in giving point,

as there is much uncertainty in thrusting at the exact place intended.

The edge of the sabre should always be kept up when giving point, for the blade may be broken or jarred from the hand by the parry, if the flat side is presented.

The shoulder should follow the thrust as far as possible, without endangering your seat in the saddle, for the purpose of holding your adversary at a greater distance, and making yourself the more secure.

If, after every thrust, you do not keep the hand as high as the head, your antagonist will get his sabre within your guard, after the parry, which he cannot do if this rule is observed.

The second point is frequently used in dismounted service with the utmost safety and effect, for your adversary gives force to the thrust by his parry. The hand, in giving this point, should not be drawn back to the hip, except in practising the first lessons, as it gives your opponent ample time to prepare for the parry.

Section IV.—*Parries.*

There should be three modes of parrying when mounted.

The *left parry* is made from the first guard, parrying from the left rear to the left front, and with the back of the sabre, immediately returning to the first guard *on your left side*, ready to repeat the parry, if necessary, or make any cut, guard, or point.

In making the parry, the hand should be kept at least as high as the shoulder—arm extended.

Were your adversary to attack on your left, or left rear, he may pass you after delivering point; and if so, he can cut *two, four,* or *six,* and from your left front guard you can receive him. After passing beyond the reach of your sabre, he can cut at your horse's head with safety, which must be guarded against by forming the left front hanging guard, well extended.

The *right parry* is also made (from the first guard on your right) from front to rear ; or, *vice versâ,* arm extended, hand as high as the shoulder, and with the back of the blade.

The parries may be made from front to rear, or rear to front on either side, when acting against *Infantry ;* but they should always be executed against cavalry so as to *beat* the point of the adversary's sabre *down.*

The action, in parrying against cavalry, should proceed alone from the wrist and shoulder.

SECTION I.—*Method of Instruction.*

As it will be indispensably necessary for the troopers to be instructed *on foot* previous to exercising in the saddle, any number, from one to fifty, can be taught the *divisions* at one time.

The company being formed in single rank and *told off* by fours, the Instructor will command:

Draw Sabre.—At the word *draw*, pass the hand over briskly to the left side, run it through the sabre-knot, turn it several times in order to secure it to the wrist, and draw the sabre about ten inches from the scabbard (holding the scabbard with the left hand at the upper ring.) At the word *sabre*, raise the arm to its full extent (throwing the point to the front as if cutting four) and bring it smartly to the right side, the back of the blade resting against the shoulder, hand at the hip, and the little finger outside of the guard or gripe. This is the position of *carry sabre.*

The sabre should not be used without having a *knot* attached to it. It enables a person to recover his weapon if forced from his grasp, and, on drills, prevents accidents which are apt to occur by the sabre escaping from the hand.

To the Front take Distance for Exercise, March.—At

the word *march*, every number *one* steps nine paces to the front; number *two*, six paces; number *three*, three paces; and number *four* remains steady; each rank dressing by its own right without command.

SECTION II.—*Proving Distance by Files.*

To the Right ; Prove Distance.—At this command, the head is turned and the arm extended to the right, point of the sabre resting on the shoulder, edge up.

Two.—At this word, the point of the sabre is extended to the right, back of the hand up and edge to the rear; the point of the sabre, the hand and shoulder horizontal.

Should the files be too close, they must take side steps to the left; the files on the right of each rank standing fast. When the files have become steady they should be commanded to *carry sabre.*

To the Front ; Prove Distance.—At this command, the hand is extended to the front, the point of the blade on the shoulder, edge up.

Two.—At this word, the point of the sabre is extended to the front, back of the hand up and edge of the blade to the right; the point of the sabre, hand and shoulder horizontal. After proving distance to the front, they should be brought to *carry sabre.*

The files being in position for exercising in the *divisions,* the Instructor commands:

First Division against Cavalry, Engage.—At the

word *engage*, the right foot is removed about eighteen inches to the right, toes turned a little inward, the left hand brought in front of the belt plate (as if holding the bridle reins), the right hand to the hip, with the back up, the thumb extended along the gripe, edge of the blade to the front, and point to the left front, at the height of the shoulder.

· *Guard.*—At this command, the arm is extended to the front, hand a little higher than the head, edge of the blade up and inclined to the front, point to the left front and about six inches higher than the hilt.

Prepare to Cut One.—At this order, the point of the sabre is thrown back over the shoulder, edge up, and the arm extended.

Cut One.—At the word *one*, the cut is made from the right to the left diagonally downward until the point of the sabre arrives in a line with the left elbow, then it is brought quickly over the left shoulder, edge up, and hand before the face.

Cut Two.—At the word *two*, the cut is made from the left to the right diagonally downward until the point arrives in a line with the right elbow, carrying the point to the rear over the right shoulder, edge up.

Cut Three.—At the word *three*, the cut is made upward from the right until the point comes in a line with the face, bringing the point briskly over the left shoulder, edge up.

Cut Four.—At the word *four*, the cut is made upward from left to right until the sabre gets in a line with the face, bringing the blade quickly over the right shoulder, point to the rear and edge to the right.

Cut Five.—At the word *five*, the cut is made from right to left horizontally, sabre brought over the left shoulder, and edge to the left.

Cut Six.—At the word *six*, the cut is made horizontally from left to right, sabre brought over the right shoulder, and edge up.

Cut Seven.—At the word *seven*, the cut is executed perpendicularly downward until the point arrives in a line with the right shoulder.

First Point.—At the word *point*, the hand is drawn back near the face, edge of the sabre up, and the hilt firmly grasped.

Two.—At the word *two*, the thrust is delivered to the front at the full extent of the arm, and edge up.

Right Rear Cut and Point.—At the word *point*, the cut *six* is made to the right rear (playing the sabre around the head), and the *first* point immediately delivered.

Right Parry.—At the word *parry*, the parry is made from front to rear, bringing the sabre over the right shoulder preparatory to cutting five left, palm of the hand up and as high as the shoulder, edge to the right and point to the rear.

Cut Five and Six.—At the word *six*, the eyes are turned to the left; the cut five is then made to the left, the blade brought behind the back, point to the right rear, and edge to the rear; the head is then turned to the right, and cut *six* is made on that side, playing the point of the sabre around the head, and returning to the *engage*.

Carry Sabre.—At this command, the sabre is brought to the shoulder as prescribed for the carry, the right foot carried to the left, and the left hand dropped to the side.

SECTION III.—*Second Division against Cavalry, Engage.*

Left Front Guard.—The arm is extended to the left front, hand a little higher than the head, point of the sabre down, and edge to the left front.

Right Front Guard.—The point of the sabre is raised (as if over the horse's neck), arm extended to the right front, hand higher than the head, and edge in the direction of the guard.

Right Guard.—The same as the right front guard, except that the arm is shifted to the right.

Right Rear Guard.—The same as right guard, but carried to the right rear.

Rear Guard.—The edge and point of the sabre to the rear, the position of the arm as in the other hanging guards.

Left Rear Guard.—This guard, when formed from the rear guard, is made by turning the palm of the hand up, keeping the point of the sabre down, and raising the arm extended over the head until the left rear hanging guard is formed, edge to the left rear.

Left Guard.—This guard is formed by bringing the sabre opposite the left shoulder, edge out.

Left Parry.—Form the first guard and parry, from rear to front, with the back of the blade, immediately preparing for the first point to the left front.

Left Front Point.—The first point is delivered to the left front as before explained.

Cut Six Right.—The cut *six* is made to the right, and the sabre brought quickly over the head to the *engage*.

SECTION IV.—*Third Division against Infantry, Engage.*

Left Front Point.—The sabre is brought in position for *first point*, the body a little inclined over to the left, from the haunches, without bending the left knee, and the point delivered downwards to the left front.

Prepare to Cut Two.—The body is inclined over to the right, sabre brought over the left shoulder, edge up, and face turned to the right front.

Cut Two.—The cut *two* is made downwards on the right side, throwing the point of the sabre to the right rear, bringing the point to the front, edge up, and the hand as high as the head, pointing to the right rear.

Cut Three.—The cut *three* is made from the rear to the right front, bringing the sabre briskly over the right shoulder, preparing to cut *one* on the left.

Cut One.—The cut *one* is made down on the left side, throwing the point of the blade to the left rear, then bringing the point to the front, edge up, and hand as high as the shoulder.

Cut Four.—The cut *four* is made from the rear to the

left front, bringing the sabre over the left shoulder, point to the rear, and the hand extended to the front ready to cut *two* on the right side.

Cut Two.—As before, playing the sabre around, ready for first point.

Give Point.—The point is made downwards to the right front, quickly forming the *first guard* on the right, ready for the right parry.

Parry.—The parry is made from the right rear to the right front with the back of the blade, bringing the sabre by the front to the left side to *first guard*, ready for left parry.

Parry.—The parry is made from the left rear to the left front, with the back of the blade, and coming to the *engage.* The instructor will command *carry sabre.*

REST.

At this command the sabre is removed from the shoulder and laid in the left elbow, edge up, the left hand placed across the right in front of the belt-plate, and the right foot drawn back about six inches. This is the position to rest when in *extended* order. When the files are close, the *left* foot is removed to the rear, back of the left hand upon the hip, and point of the sabre resting upon the toe of the boot, edge to the right, and hand resting upon the knob of the hilt.

ATTENTION.

At this command the sabre is thrown to the front (as

if cutting four) and brought to a carry. The men, in every other respect, take the position of the soldier.

If the files are close, the point of the sabre is merely raised to the carry, and the position of the soldier resumed.

Section V.—*Returning Sabre.*

Return Sabre.—At the word *return*, the sabre is passed across the breast (from a carry) so that the hilt will touch the left shoulder, edge to the front, and point up, immediately letting the point fall to the rear, then raising the hand as high as the head, passing the side of the blade close to the arm, and returning it within ten inches of the hilt.

Sabre.—At the word *sabre*, push it to the hilt, free the right hand from the sabre-knot, and drop it to the side.

Section VI.—*Manual Exercise.*

The company being paraded in single rank, the instructor will command:

Draw sabre.	(As before directed.)	
Tell off by fours from the right.	"	"
To the front, take distance for exercise.	"	"
To the right, prove distance.	"	"
To the front, prove distance.	"	"
Carry sabre	"	"

When the company is thus prepared, it will be exercised in the following manner :

SECTION VII.—*Divisions.*

WORDS OF COMMAND.

First Division against Cavalry, Engage.—Guard, prepare to cut one.   Cut one, two, three, four, five, six, seven. Front give point, two.   Right rear, cut and point. Right parry.   Cut five left, and six right.   Carry sabre.

Second Division against Cavalry, Engage. — Left front guard.   Right front guard.   Right guard.   Right rear guard.   Rear guard.   Left rear guard.   Left guard, prepare for left parry.   Parry.   Left front give point. cut six right.   Carry sabre.

Third Division against Infantry, Engage.—Left front give point.   Prepare to cut two.   Cut two, three, *Change.*   Cut one, four, two, and point to the right. Right parry.   Left parry.   Carry sabre.   Rest.

SECTION I.—*Attack and Defence, Dismounted.*

AFTER the men are well instructed in the cavalry divisions, they will prepare for *attack* and *defence*, as follows :

Prepare for Attack and Defence.—At the word *defence*, every file will *half face* to the left, placing the heel of the right foot against the hollow of the left, the sabre at a carry.

Guard.—At the word *guard*, throw the weight of the body on the left leg, slightly bending the knee, advance the right foot about six inches, place the back of the left hand on the hip, incline the upper part of the body well forward, and form the *first* guard as before explained.

ATTACK.

Cut One.—At this command, advance the right foot so far as to straighten the left leg without removing the foot from the ground, and cut one at antagonist's left cheek, keeping the point of the blade on a horizontal line with the hand and shoulder.

DEFENCE.

Second Guard.—At the word *guard*, draw back the right foot to within six inches of the left, and form the *second guard*, hand a little higher than the head, arm to the full extent and to the left front, and point of the blade dropped, eyeing your adversary under the sword arm.

The reader will bear in mind that the hanging guards (numbers two and three) are formed to the right and left, and the point of the sabre raised or lowered according to the manner and force of the cut. If the cuts are made diagonally downwards, or horizontally, the point of the blade should be raised; but, if diagonally upwards, the point must be dropped.

ATTACK.

Cut Two.—At the word *two*, step out, as in cut *one*, and cut two at your adversary's right cheek, point of the blade, hand and shoulder horizontal.*

DEFENCE.

Third Guard.—At this command, draw back the right foot (as explained in second guard) and form the *third guard* to the right front, hand higher than the head, arm extended, and point of the blade out.

As this guard (protecting against cut two) constrains the body somewhat, the first guard, carried a little to the right, is preferable; and from this position, cuts *four* and

---

* When the file is in the attitude of cutting or thrusting (the right foot advanced), the leg, from the knee down, should be straight.

six can be guarded against by dropping the point, and without varying the hand to the right or left.

We deem it proper to observe here, that in the *standing guards* (point of the blade up) the force of the cut must be sustained by the wrist alone; but, in the hanging guards, the shoulder receives the shock.

ATTACK.

Cut Three.—At this command, cut *three* at antagonist's left side, right or left arm, forming *first guard* immediately.

DEFENCE.

Second Guard.—At this command, form the *second* guard (as before explained) point of the blade *in*.

ATTACK.

Cut Four.—At this command, cut four at adversary's sword arm.

In making the cuts three and four the hand should never be below the shoulder.

DEFENCE.

Third Guard.—At this order, form the third guard by dropping the point, arm extended.

In all guards, care must be observed to receive the cuts on the *fort*, not the *feeble* of the blade.

The *fort* is that portion of the sabre from the hilt towards the point which enables you to resist all cuts, and parry all points without much exertion. The *feeble* is the part of the blade near the point, by which you are unable to ward off a thrust, guard a cut, or force your adversary's blade.

Cut Five.—At this command, cut five at antagonist's neck.

DEFENCE.

Second Guard.—Form the second guard (as before explained) to protect against cut *one*.

ATTACK.

Cut Six.—At this command, cut *six* at adversary's neck.

DEFENCE.

Third Guard.—Form *first* or *third* guard, as explained, to protect against cut *two*.

ATTACK.

Cut Seven.—At this command, cut *seven* on the adversary's head.

DEFENCE.

First Guard.—Form *first* guard.

ATTACK.

First Point.—At this command, bring the sabre in position for *first* point.

Two.—At this word, the thrust should be delivered with force, and the hand raised as high as the head as soon as the point is given.

DEFENCE.

Parry.—At this order, the first guard is formed.

Two.—At the word *two*, the parry will be made downwards to the right with the back of the blade, returning to the first guard.

The parry may be made to the front and at the same time returning the thrust.

ATTACK.

Second Point.—At this command, the sabre is brought back, right hand on the hip (as explained in *mounted service*).

Two.—At this word, deliver the point at antagonist's breast, raising the hand as high as the shoulder.

This point will be more effective by sinking upon the left knee and delivering it upwards against your adversary's breast; for, in the ordinary or *natural* parry downwards to the right side, your adversary's blade will slide harmlessly to your hilt. If your antagonist parries with force, incline the hand a little to the left without altering the direction of the point.

DEFENCE.

Parry.—At this command, form the *first* guard.

Two.—At the word *two*, parry the thrust by keeping the hand before the face, and describing a circle from right to left, or left to right, according to the manner the point is delivered.

Carry Sabre.

Front Face.
Rest, or Return Sabre.

Section II.

When the men are sufficiently practised in the attack and defence, the company will again be formed in single rank (by the command, form rank, march), and told off by *twos.* The number *ones* will advance six paces and halt. The files will prove distance to the right (as before explained), and the front rank or number *ones* will about face. The instructor should then attack them singly in order to ascertain if they take position, and make the guards and parries properly.

Whether the cuts are made separately or collectively, the invariable rule of keeping the hand directed to the antagonist's left ear must be observed, and care taken to avoid carrying the sword hand to the right of the head previous to making cuts *one, three,* and *five,* which exposes the body to a return of the same cuts. Upon the same principle, the hand should not be carried to the left when preparing to cut *two, four,* or *six.*

The right foot should be advanced in all cuts and points (as explained in cut one), and in the guards and parries; re-take position as in second guard, keeping sight of the adversary's eye.

It should be observed that the safety and advantage in giving point is in advancing the shoulder with the arm, and inclining the body well forward, showing only your right side to the antagonist.

The *point* should never be made except when it can be applied without risk ; for, if it is parried with force, it is difficult to recover the guard in time.

The guards protecting against cuts *three* and *four* may be lowered somewhat, but not so much as to guard cuts made below the knee : if your adversary should cut *three* or *four* at the leg, draw it back and cut his sword arm or head before he recovers his position.

Feints.—The *feint* is a mock assault of a cut or thrust, and is done by a cut or thrust *feigned* at one place and made at another.

The feint is practised only when in position for guarding or parrying, and the *cut* or *thrust* instantly follows, advancing the right foot as explained.

SECTION III.—*Words of Command in the Attack and Defence.*

Prepare for Attack and Defence.—Guard. Cut one, second guard. Cut two, first or third guard. Cut three, second guard. Cut four, third guard. Cut five, second guard. Cut six, third or first guard. Cut seven, first guard. First point, two, parry. Second point, two, parry. Carry sabre. Front face.

Two persons should take position (as in *prepare for attack and defence*), facing each other, and measure the distance by extending the arms and blades horizontally, so that the points of the sabres touch each other's hilts, then put themselves in attitude for guarding, cutting and pointing, guarding and parrying, alternately, in the above order.

After the parties are expert in the attack and defence *without removing their left feet from the ground,* the one on the defensive may retire a step or two at each cut or thrust guarding or parrying at the same time; the attacking party continuing the advance, and preserving the proper distance.

Lesson I.—*Fencing in the Saddle.*

(*See Plate* XXVIII.)

In this practice, two persons should be mounted, and about three feet apart, sword arm to sword arm. The horses being side to side (with their heads in opposite directions) the riders should cross sabres by forming the *first* guard to the right.

In this position they will endeavor to preserve *cutting distance* and describe a circle slowly, *without disengaging sabres.*

When they become proficient in this, the pace may be increased.

Lesson II.

(*See Plate* XXIX.)

The riders take position as in the first lesson, the one turning his horse upon his own centre, while the other describes a circle around him; first at a walk, then gradually increasing the pace.

Great care should be observed not to enlarge nor diminish the circle lest the sabres become disengaged, thereby rendering it necessary to re-commence the movement; the great object being always to be within cutting distance.

After being sufficiently expert in describing the circle and keeping the proper distance, the one should endeavor to gain the other's left rear or "weak quarter" by quickening the pace. The one acting on the defensive must keep sword arm to sword arm with his adversary by turning his horse upon his own centre.

The reader will, in this case, perceive the advantage of acting on the defensive.

Lesson III.

(*See Plate* XXX.)

The riders take position side to side, horses' heads in the same direction, both forming the *first* guard (one on the left side, the other on the right, sabres crossed), and move at the walk, then the trot, and lastly the gallop.

The rider with the first guard formed, or first cut made on his right, is the attacking party, and should occasionally urge or check his horse for the purpose of gaining the advantage of his adversary. The one on the defensive should keep pace with his antagonist.

In the pursuit, the skilful horseman always attacks at the left rear, for he has the advantage of the width of his opponent's chest, and may cut or thrust with impunity.

In order to avoid the attack at this point, the defensive party should turn his horse immediately to the "right about" and receive his pursuer sword arm to sword arm;

Plate XXVIII.—Two Persons engaged in the First Lesson of Fencing in the Saddle.

Plate XXIX.—Two Persons engaged in the Second Lesson of Fencing in the Saddle.

Plate XXX.—Two Persons engaged in the Third Lesson of Fencing in the Saddle.

or, when the attacking party has gained the left rear, suddenly check the horse that he may pass, and then pursue him.

If there is any circumstance which would prevent him doing either, he should, after receiving his antagonist on the left side, turn his horse to the "left about" on his fore legs, giving the left spur vigorously (to make him pass his croup around) and at the same time protect his head by extending the guard.

In these lessons the parties should attack and defend alternately.

FINIS.

Made in the USA
Middletown, DE
28 December 2024